EXPLORING THE
SOUTHWEST

BY TAMMY GAGNE

CONTENT CONSULTANT
Santiago Guerra, PhD
Visiting Assistant Professor of Southwest Studies
Colorado College

Core Library

Cover image: Cacti grow on buttes such as this one in
Hewitt Canyon, Arizona.

An Imprint of Abdo Publishing
abdopublishing.com

abdopublishing.com

Published by Abdo Publishing, a division of ABDO, PO Box 398166, Minneapolis, Minnesota 55439. Copyright © 2018 by Abdo Consulting Group, Inc. International copyrights reserved in all countries. No part of this book may be reproduced in any form without written permission from the publisher. Core Library™ is a trademark and logo of Abdo Publishing.

Printed in the United States of America, North Mankato, Minnesota
102017
012018

Cover Photo: Anton Foltin/Shutterstock Images
Interior Photos: Anton Foltin/Shutterstock Images, 1; Shutterstock Images, 4–5, 18–19, 24–25, 39; Red Line Editorial, 7; Underwood Archives/Archive Photos/Getty Images, 10–11; MPI/Archive Photos/Getty Images, 13; Nick Fox/Shutterstock Images, 22–23; Roberto Lo Savio/iStockphoto, 28; Roschetzky Photography/Shutterstock Images, 30–31; Ross D. Franklin/AP Images, 33; iStockphoto, 35; Witold Skrypczak/Lonely Planet Images/Getty Images, 36–37

Editor: Megan Ellis
Imprint Designer: Maggie Villaume
Series Design Direction: Ryan Gale

Publisher's Cataloging-in-Publication Data

Names: Gagne, Tammy, author.
Title: Exploring the Southwest / by Tammy Gagne.
Description: Minneapolis, Minnesota : Abdo Publishing, 2018. | Series: Exploring America's regions | Includes online resources and index.
Identifiers: LCCN 2017946945 | ISBN 9781532113840 (lib.bdg.) | ISBN 9781532152726 (ebook)
Subjects: LCSH: Southwest, Old--Juvenile literature. | Discovery and exploration--Juvenile literature. | Travel--Juvenile literature. | United States--Historical geography--Juvenile literature.
Classification: DDC 917.90--dc23
LC record available at https://lccn.loc.gov/2017946945

CONTENTS

CHAPTER ONE

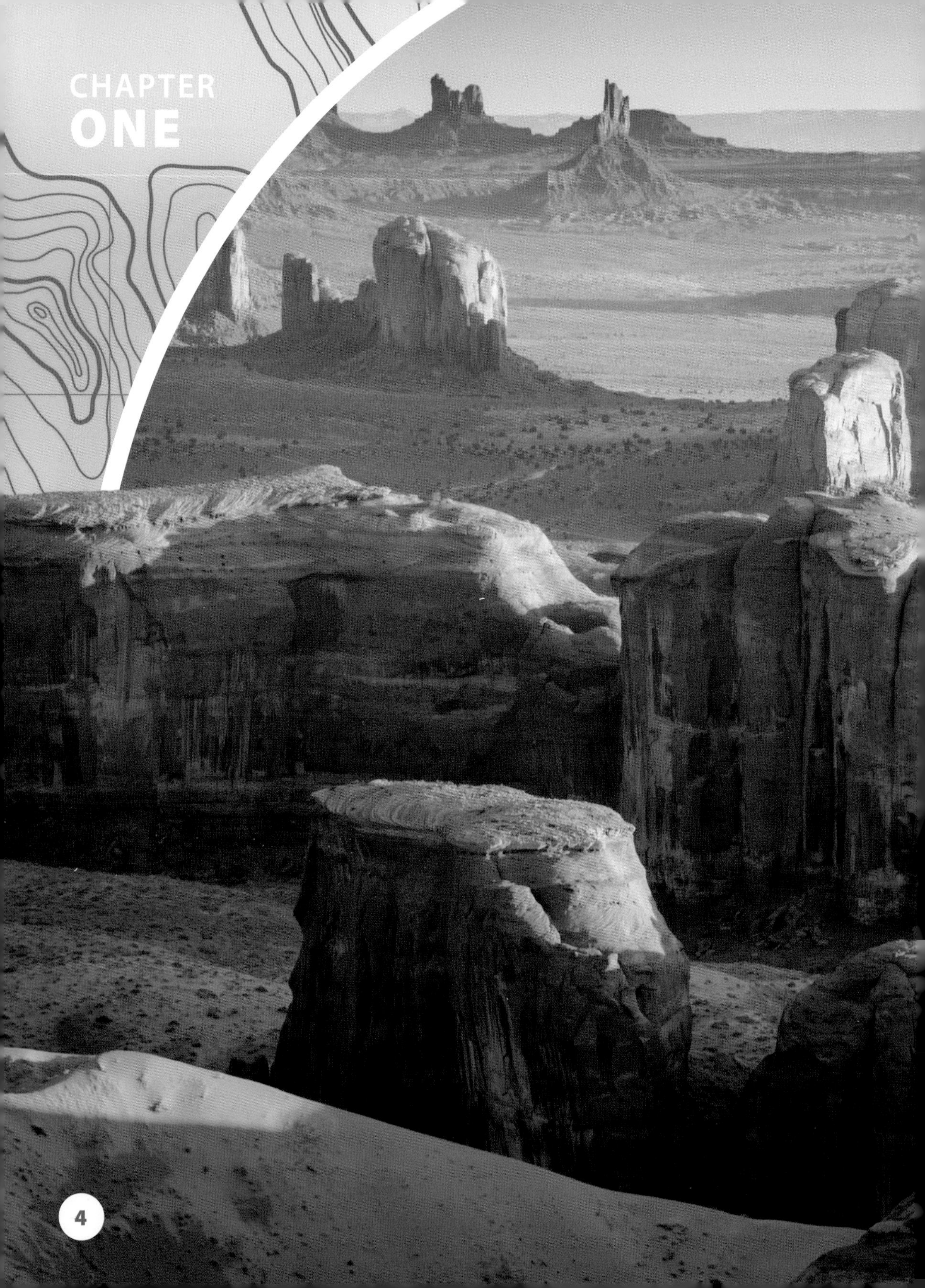

WELCOME TO THE SOUTHWEST

America's Southwest has many great views. The grasslands of the Great Plains range from Oklahoma to Texas. Wheat, corn, and cotton grow on this flat, fertile land. Sandy deserts, high plateaus, and deep canyons cover New Mexico and Arizona.

The Southwest covers approximately 564,700 square miles (907,670 sq km). It includes four US states. Three of these states were the last ones added to the contiguous

Arizona's Monument Valley is one of the Southwest's many beautiful landscapes.

CHANGES IN THE AIR

The dry climate of the Southwest is becoming even drier. Low-pressure air patterns in the North Pacific Ocean bring needed rain. But they have started to happen less often. In recent years, high-pressure patterns have been more common. This change has brought much less rain. It has caused droughts.

United States. But this land has a history much older than that of the nation itself. Native American tribes have lived in this region for thousands of years.

THE SOUTHWESTERN CLIMATE

The Southwest is the hottest and driest region in the United States. The average high temperature of Tucson, Arizona, is 83 degrees Fahrenheit (28°C). It gets an average rainfall of only 11.6 inches (29.5 cm) per year.

But not all parts of the Southwest are sunny all the time. It rains a lot in eastern Texas and Oklahoma. The city of Lufkin, Texas, gets an average of 49 inches (124 cm) of rainfall each year. Severe thunderstorms are common in these areas. Tornadoes happen there too.

THE SOUTHWEST REGION

Chapter One discusses the size of the states in the Southwest region. This map shows the area's cities, vast deserts, and long rivers. Does this map match your understanding of the region from the text? Why or why not?

SOUTHWEST CITIES AND TOWNS

More than 31 million people live in the Southwest. The largest city is Houston, Texas. Other large cities include Phoenix, Arizona; Albuquerque, New Mexico; and Oklahoma City, Oklahoma.

Many of the Southwest's towns have a lot of history and culture. German and Austrian pioneers settled in

Schulenburg, Texas. It is home to the Texas Polka Music Museum. Broken Bow, Oklahoma, has many tourist spots, such as Broken Bow Lake and the Ouachita National Forest. Jerome, Arizona, has an elevation of 4,948 feet (1,508 m). It has the nickname "America's Most Vertical City." People have enjoyed mineral hot springs in Jemez Springs, New Mexico, for almost 4,000 years. Peaceful areas and exciting larger cities bring people to the Southwest.

PERSPECTIVES

THE MOST VERTICAL CITY

Jerome was a copper mining town. It produced more than 3 million pounds (1.36 million kg) of copper per month. It became a ghost town when the mine closed. Artists started living there in the 1960s. Today, Jerome is home to many artists. Watercolor painter Anne Bassett has a gallery in Jerome. She says, "I am enormously proud that people from around the world have told me they came to Jerome after seeing its charm in my drawings."

STRAIGHT TO THE
SOURCE

Actor Jim Parsons stars in the television show *The Big Bang Theory*. He is from Houston. He explains that Houston is not always the way people picture it:

> *I get asked more often than I would imagine questions about what it's like in Houston, and several people have asked if there are lots of horses. What's funny is . . . I saw more horses in New York than I ever saw in Houston. . . . I saw more art in Houston than I ever saw in New York. There can be a [wrong] notion of tumbleweeds and cowboys and there are some, but not rolling down Montrose [a street in Houston].*

Source: Jim Parsons. "My Houston." *VisitHouston*. Greater Houston Convention & Visitors Bureau, n.d. Web. Accessed July 5, 2017.

What's the Big Idea?
Read the primary source above carefully. What is the main idea? Make a list of two or three details that support this idea.

A LONG HISTORY

Texas was added to the United States in 1845. The other three states in the Southwest were added in the early 1900s. But the Southwest region has a much longer history. Several Native American tribes lived in the area as early as 11,000 BCE.

The Apache lived in what are now the states of Arizona, New Mexico, and Oklahoma. These nomadic people hunted to live. Pueblo tribal groups, such as the Hopi and Taos Indians, settled in modern-day Arizona, New Mexico, and Texas. They lived in clay houses called adobes. They grew vegetables

The distinctive homes of the Pueblo tribal groups have stood for centuries in the Southwest.

and cotton. The Navajo settled nearby. They learned how to grow corn and weave cotton into blankets.

WAR AND WATER

The US government took the land of the Cherokee nation in 1838 and 1839. It was east of the Mississippi River. President Andrew Jackson's policy made the Cherokee people leave their homes. They were moved to the Oklahoma territory. Their journey was difficult and long. Many people didn't survive. The journey is called the Trail of Tears. It was only the beginning. The US government continued to take land from Native Americans by force.

PUEBLO-INSPIRED ARCHITECTURE

The influence of the Pueblo tribal groups can be seen in many buildings in the Southwest. Pueblo-inspired architecture is sometimes called Pueblo Revival. It has flat roofs and thick walls. The walls are made of sun-dried mud. This helps keep buildings cool. Some builders use concrete. This produces a similar result.

US troops attacked fortresses within Mexico during the Mexican-American War (1846–1848).

As the United States grew, the nation's relationship with Mexico became worse. Texas declared independence from Mexico in 1836. The United States annexed Texas in 1845. But there was a problem. The United States and Mexico both wanted the land between the Rio Grande and the Nueces rivers.

US troops mobilized near the Rio Grande. In response, Mexico attacked the troops. On May 13, 1846, the United States and Mexico went to war. The war lasted for two years. After the conflict, the two nations signed the Treaty of Guadalupe Hidalgo. This treaty allowed the United States to purchase the remaining land west of Texas. By the end of the war, Mexico had lost approximately one-half of its territory.

The war with Mexico was not the only fighting in the Southwest in the 1800s. The United States expanded railroad transportation. New railroads were built in the Southwest in the 1860s. They went through Native American territories. The United States took Native Americans from their homes. Many fought back. These American Indian Wars were especially violent.

As people migrated to the Southwest, water became an important issue. People need fresh water in such a dry region. Dams were built to make life easier for settlers. But people argued over who had rights to the water from many rivers. Debates about water continue in the region today.

MAJOR HISTORICAL EVENTS OF THE SOUTHWEST

The 1889 Land Run was a government act. It made 2 million more acres (809,371 ha) available for settlers in the Southwest. Families in the eastern United States loaded their things into covered wagons. They headed west. They claimed their own land in this

PERSPECTIVES
NO PLACE LIKE HOME

Former Cornell University president Elizabeth Garrett was born in Oklahoma City in 1963. Garrett had a deep connection to her home state:

My mother's family arrived when the state was Indian Territory, working as schoolteachers. My father's family came during the Oklahoma Land Run. Oklahoma has . . . roots that include egalitarian ideals, a belief in the value of education, and a sense that anything can be accomplished by hard work and creative intelligence. The prairie landscape provides a sense of limitless opportunity.

new territory. The arrangement helped both the settlers and the government. Many people could now afford their own property. The government made money from them. But Native Americans suffered greatly. The Land Run violated some treaties. The US government had said it would not take land that belonged to the tribes.

In the 1930s, severe dust storms called the Dust Bowl struck plains in the Southwest. High winds and a lot of dust killed many people and animals. The dangerous storms drove many settlers away.

The National Aeronautics and Space Administration (NASA) started the Space Task Group in Houston in 1958. It oversaw manned space flight programs. It supervised space missions. This included the first moon landing in 1969. The site was renamed approximately four years later. It is now called the Johnson Space Center because of US president Lyndon B. Johnson. Johnson, who was from Texas, was a dedicated supporter of the space program.

STRAIGHT TO THE
SOURCE

Jeff Haozous is the chairman of the Fort Sill Apache Tribe in Oklahoma. He explained in an interview how Geronimo, one of the most well-known members of the Apache tribe, handled the relocation of the tribe:

> *In the late 1800s Chiricahua and Warm Springs [Apache] reservations in Arizona and New Mexico were closed, and the tribe was moved to the San Carlos Apache Reservation in eastern Arizona. . . . Fearing for his life, Geronimo . . . left the reservation. This started a conflict with the United States that led to the imprisonment of our people and their removal from the Southwest to Florida, then Alabama, and finally to Fort Sill in Oklahoma, where they were released in 1914. This nearly 28-year imprisonment is one of the most significant eras in our history.*

> Source: Dennis Zotigh. "Meet Native America: Jeff Haozous, Chairman of the Fort Sill Apache Tribe." *National Museum of the American Indian.* Smithsonian Institution, July 28, 2016. Web. Accessed July 5, 2017.

Changing Minds

Imagine you were alive when Apache tribe members were forced from their reservations. How would you speak out against their imprisonment? Make sure you explain your opinion. Include facts and details that support your reasons.

FAMOUS LANDMARKS AND WATERWAYS

Many Southwest landforms look like giant sculptures. Rivers carved deep gorges in the Southwest. The biggest of these is the Grand Canyon in Arizona. It is 277 miles (446 km) long, up to 18 miles (29 km) wide, and more than a mile (1.6 km) deep. Visitors can see its amazing views. Some ride in helicopters above the massive canyon. Others hike or ride mules to

The Colorado River twists and turns through the Grand Canyon, creating recognizable landmarks such as Horseshoe Bend.

its very bottom. Some visitors even walk out on a glass skywalk to see the canyon below them.

BARRINGER METEOR CRATER

A giant meteor struck Earth approximately 50,000 years ago near Winslow, Arizona. The hole it made is known as the Barringer Meteor Crater. Daniel Moreau Barringer was an engineer. He discovered that a meteor created the crater. The crater is almost one mile (1.6 km) wide and more than 550 feet (167 m) deep. Tourists can look down into the crater from the rim.

The Colorado River created the Grand Canyon. It flows 1,450 miles (2,334 km) through the Southwest. It supplies 30 million people with water for drinking, bathing, and recreation.

The Rio Grande flows 1,900 miles (3,058 km) through Colorado, New Mexico, and Texas. It forms a border between Texas and Mexico. It empties into the Gulf of Mexico. In some parts of the Rio Grande Gorge, the river passes through 800-foot (244-m) chasms.

MAN-MADE LANDMARKS OF THE SOUTHWEST

People have made many landmarks in the Southwest. One of the oldest is Montezuma Castle in Campe Verde, Arizona. It was built by the Sinagua people in the 1100s CE. It is 100 feet (30 m) above the ground. The ruins aren't safe for people to enter. Instead visitors view them from the trail below.

Another famous landmark is Taos Pueblo in New Mexico.

PERSPECTIVES

AN EDUCATIONAL TRIP

Route 66 is one of the most popular ways to travel through the Southwest. Bobby Troup wrote a famous song about the highway in 1946. His wife came up with the idea. They were looking at a map while planning a trip to California. He said:

She looked at it and she said, 'Why don't you write a song about Route 40?' And I said, 'Well, that's really kind of silly, because we're going to pick up Route 66 right outside of Chicago and then take it all the way into Los Angeles.' So we're driving along, and she said, 'Get your kicks on Route 66.' Her words became the song's trademark lyrics.

Artists update Cadillac Ranch with new layers of spray paint.

Taos Indians live in this traditional pueblo-style settlement. Visitors can take a guided tour of the pueblo. Some structures now have art galleries and artisan shops.

One of the oddest southwestern landmarks is in Amarillo, Texas. Cadillac Ranch is a work of art along

a famous highway called Route 66. The artists put ten Cadillac automobiles in the sand. The cars get the attention of travelers. They range from a 1949 Club Sedan to a 1963 Sedan de Ville. Approximately half of each car sits above the ground.

THE WILDLIFE OF THE SOUTHWEST

Some people may not know that the Southwest has many types of wildlife. Plants and animals in this region must be very hardy to live in the harsh conditions.

ANIMALS OF THE SOUTHWEST

One of the toughest southwestern animals is the coyote. It is related to the dogs that people keep as pets. Coyotes can eat many things, such as rabbits and squirrels. If they cannot find these, coyotes will eat reptiles instead.

Coyotes may look like domestic dogs, but they are fierce predators in the Southwest.

BEAUTY IN THE DESERT

Cherie Ann Gossett is a botanical artist from the Southwest. She painted a chitalpa for the 15th Annual International American Society of Botanical Artists in New York. This tree has flowers. It grows to between 20 and 30 feet (6 to 9 m) tall. It blooms from May to September. Gossett explained,

Other than cacti, many desert plants don't produce large flowers. The challenge is to portray plants in paintings which will catch the eye and that people will enjoy and appreciate . . . . I find myself picking subjects like native hibiscus, Desert Willow, and the Chitalpa which all have relatively striking flowers.

Bighorn sheep live in the Southwest too. Like coyotes, they find ways to live in the desert. They do not need to drink water every day. In the summer, bighorn sheep drink water every three days. In the winter, they do not need to drink at all. They get enough water from the plants they eat.

One of the most unusual creatures of the Southwest is the roadrunner. Like the Looney Tunes character, this bird is fast. It can run up to 17 miles per hour (27 km/h). The species may not look fierce, but it can kill and eat venomous rattlesnakes.

PLANTS OF THE SOUTHWEST

Plants of the Southwest can protect themselves. The desert spoon is found in Arizona, New Mexico, and Texas. It has hundreds of long, thin leaves. Each leaf is lined with small teeth. They protect the inner part of the plant from hungry animals.

The prickly pear cactus is found in southwestern deserts. The plant's name is a good description for it. Large spines protect the plant's fruit. Both the fruit and the

MORE THAN DESERT

Not all of the Southwest is a desert. Flat grasslands called steppes are common in northern Arizona and northern New Mexico. Steppes are not as dry as deserts. Grasses such as blue grama and western wheatgrass grow there. Shrubs such as sagebrush also grow well on steppes.

EXPLORE ONLINE

Chapter Four discusses plants that grow in the Southwest. The article below talks about one of these species. How is the information from the article the same as the information in Chapter Four? What new information did you learn from the article?

TO SAVE SAGEBRUSH, RESEARCHERS UNLEASH THE POWER OF SHEEP

abdocorelibrary.com/exploring-southwest

branches, called paddles, can be eaten. They are even sold in grocery stores.

Sagebrush is also found in the Southwest's deserts. This shrub grows best in a dry environment. Some Native people use sagebrush to treat certain illnesses and disinfect wounds. It can even be used to treat snake bites.

The spines on a prickly pear cactus make the fruit difficult to harvest.

INDUSTRY IN THE SOUTHWEST

The Southwest has many industries. They include technology, energy, and tourism. These industries create many jobs. They provide goods and services for people both inside and outside the region.

TECHNOLOGY

Technology is a large global industry. Dell, Intel, and Texas Instruments are only a few of the technology companies in the Southwest. Dell is in Round Rock, Texas. It makes personal

Solar panels outside Austin, Texas, provide electricity for thousands of homes.

Technology companies need employees with knowledge in science, technology, engineering, and math (STEM). Jari Askins is the former lieutenant governor of Oklahoma. He was interviewed about the program Project Lead the Way. It encourages people to study STEM. He said,

A lot of those positions [in Oklahoma] end up being filled by students coming from other states because we have not generated that base of interest in our own students. Programs like this can grow our own future workforce.

computers. Intel makes computer processors for many computer companies. It is the largest employer in Chandler, Arizona. Texas Instruments makes semiconductors. These are used in many types of electronic equipment, such as cell phones, computers, and digital cameras.

ENERGY

People use energy to power different types of technology. Much of this energy comes from nonrenewable

fossil fuels such as oil and gasoline. But these sources of energy add pollution to the environment.

Renewable sources help lower pollution. One source of renewable energy is the sun. The sun shines for approximately 300 days each year in the Southwest. More than 100 solar energy companies are located in the state of Arizona alone.

Another type of renewable energy is wind. Companies such as British Petroleum (BP) use this natural resource to make and store energy. BP is one of the world's largest fossil fuel companies. But it now has four wind farms in Texas. They create enough energy to power 157,000 homes.

TOURISM

Many people visit the Southwest for its powerful history and beautiful landmarks. Approximately 266 million people came to Texas from other US states in 2016. Businesses such as restaurants and hotels are important to the Southwest's economy.

Visitors to Arizona spent $21 billion in 2016. Tourism was the state's top industry that year. The Grand Canyon is one of the largest tourist attractions in the world. That is why Arizona is called the "Grand Canyon State."

THE POWER OF
THE SUN

Texas receives a lot of sunshine. In one month, the sun could provide more energy than all of the oil that has been harvested in the state's history. People use this energy by putting solar panels on their homes. DC energy, which is used to charge batteries, is changed to AC energy at a converter box. The electronic devices in our homes use AC energy. Looking at this diagram, why do you think people might want to use solar energy? How is it different from using fossil fuels?

1. SOLAR PANELS CONVERT SUNLIGHT INTO DC ELECTRICITY.

2. THE DC ELECTRICITY IS TURNED INTO AC ELECTRICITY THAT OUR HOMES CAN USE.

3. THE SOLAR ELECTRICITY CONNECTS TO THE HOUSE'S WIRING AT THE FUSE BOX.

5. THE HOUSE IS POWERED BY SOLAR ELECTRICITY.

4. EXTRA SOLAR POWER CAN BE SOLD BACK TO THE ELECTRIC COMPANY.

THE PEOPLES AND CULTURES OF THE SOUTHWEST

Large numbers of Anglo-Americans, Native Americans, Hispanic Americans, and immigrants live in the Southwest. Together, their histories and traditions make up the area's unique culture.

HISPANIC CULTURE

Hispanic culture is found throughout the Southwest. In 1598, the Spanish settled what is now New Mexico. Today, New Mexico is

Shops on El Paso Street in El Paso, Texas, display signs in both Spanish and English.

nearly 49 percent Hispanic or Latino. Texas is 39 percent Hispanic or Latino.

Arizona, New Mexico, and Texas are among the top Spanish-speaking states. Many people in this region learned the language as part of their own culture. People in this region have been speaking Spanish even longer than English. This is because the southwestern states were once a part of Mexico. The variety of Spanish in the Southwest also contains words from native tribes.

PERSPECTIVES
UP, UP, AND AWAY!

Every October people from around the world visit New Mexico for the Albuquerque International Balloon Fiesta. More than 500 balloons fly over the city in the nine-day event. It is the largest festival of its kind in the world. Pilot Glenn Moyer has said the annual event is a lot of fun: "Albuquerque is ballooning. Really, it's the world's largest event. Who wouldn't want to be a star on that stage?"

Two Navajo women sit outside their hogan, a traditional Navajo dwelling.

KEEPING WITH TRADITION

Native American tribes in the Southwest region sell colorful handmade baskets. These tribes have used the same method to weave them for thousands of years.

Baskets with similar patterns have been found dating back to 6000 BCE. In the past, they stored corn and beans. Now, they are often made as decorations.

NATIVE AMERICAN CULTURE

The Navajo Nation is the most populous Native American reservation in the United States. It has more than 250,000 members. Their traditions, including jewelry making and music, have become part of the broader culture of the Southwest.

Most Navajo tribe members speak English. But the Navajo have also kept their own culture. Many members still speak the Navajo language and practice their traditional religion.

IMMIGRATION

The Southwest is the fastest-growing region in the United States. Houston grew by more than 400,000 people between 2000 and 2010. This was due to immigration. Houston added 4,818 refugees to this number in 2014. They came from 40 different nations. Students in Houston's public schools now speak more than 100 languages.

Because of its rich cultural history, beautiful landmarks, and amazing wildlife, it's no wonder why so many people love to visit and live in the Southwest.

FURTHER EVIDENCE

Chapter Six discusses the peoples and cultures of the Southwest. What is one of the main ideas of this chapter? What key evidence supports this idea? Take a look at the website below. Find information from the site that supports the main idea of this chapter. Does the information support an existing piece of evidence in the chapter, or does it add new evidence?

WELCOME TO THE NAVAJO NATION GOVERNMENT

abdocorelibrary.com/exploring-southwest

FAST FACTS

- Total Area: 564,700 square miles (907,670 sq km)

- Population: 40.8 million

- Largest City: Houston, Texas

- Largest State by Population: Texas

- Smallest State by Population: New Mexico

- Largest State by Land Size: Texas

- Smallest State by Land Size: Oklahoma

- Highest Point: Wheeler Peak in New Mexico, 13,161 feet (4,011 m) above sea level

- Lowest Point: Gulf Coast, at sea level

- Landmark: The Grand Canyon contains fossils of ancient marine animals that are 1.2 billion years old.

- Deserts: The Chihuahuan Desert covers 200 million acres (80.9 million ha) across the American Southwest, as well as parts of the country of Mexico.

STOP AND
THINK

Tell the Tale

Chapter One of this book discusses the states that make up the Southwest. Imagine that you are planning a weeklong road trip to this region. Which states would you want to visit first? What attractions would interest you most? Write 200 words about the things you would want to do and see in this region.

Dig Deeper

After reading this book, what questions do you still have about the Southwest region? Find a few reliable sources that will help you answer these questions. Write a paragraph about what you learn in this process.

Take a Stand

Chapter Six discusses immigration to the Southwest. Many immigrants to this region speak Spanish. Do you think it is important for everyone in the Southwest to learn Spanish? Write an essay about your opinion. Use evidence to support your answer.

Surprise Me

Chapter Four discusses animals and plants found in the Southwest region. After reading this book, what facts about them surprised you the most? Write a few sentences about each one. Why did you find them surprising?

GLOSSARY

annex
to add to a nation's territory

architecture
the study and design
of buildings

chasm
a deep opening in the
earth's surface

contiguous
touching or connected

egalitarian
relating to the belief that all
people are equal

fossil fuels
nonrenewable energy
sources that were created
in the course of millions
of years

gorge
a narrow valley between
high, rocky walls

nomadic
moving from one place to
another instead of settling in
one location

refugee
a person forced to leave a
country to escape harm from
war or a natural disaster

semiconductor
an essential part of most
electronic devices

tumbleweed
a plant that breaks apart
from where it grew and
moves away in the wind

venomous
the ability to release poison

ONLINE RESOURCES

To learn more about the southwestern region of the United States, visit our free resource websites below.

Visit **abdocorelibrary.com** for free Common Core resources for teachers and students, including vetted activities, multimedia, and booklinks, for deeper subject comprehension.

Visit **abdobooklinks.com** for free additional online weblinks for further learning. These links are routinely monitored and updated to provide the most current information available.

LEARN MORE

Stewart, J. J. *Grand Canyon National Park*. Minneapolis, MN: Abdo Publishing, 2017.

Conley, Kate. *Solar Energy*. Minneapolis, MN: Abdo Publishing, 2017.

INDEX

About the Author

Tammy Gagne has authored dozens of books for both adults and children. She has written about culture, geography, and nature conservation. She lives in northern New England with her husband, son, and pets.